Scaling Up

Ricardo Rodriguez

Contents

Introduction to scaling up

What is scaling up?

Scaling up is the process of increasing the size or capacity of a business in order to achieve sustained growth. It can be done by expanding into new markets, launching new products or services, or increasing production.

Scaling up is often seen as a desirable goal for businesses, as it can lead to increased revenue, profitability, and market share. However, it is important to note that scaling up also comes with challenges, such as the need to maintain quality control, manage costs effectively, and adapt to new markets.

Here is a more detailed explanation of the scaling up process:

1. **Define your goals:** What do you want to achieve by scaling up? Do you want to increase revenue, profitability, market share, or something else? Once you know your goals, you can develop a plan to achieve them.

2. **Assess your current capabilities:** What are your strengths and weaknesses? What resources do you have available? It is

important to have a realistic understanding of your capabilities before you start scaling up.

3. **Identify your target market**: Who are you trying to reach with your products or services? Where are they located? What are their needs and wants? Once you know your target market, you can develop strategies to reach them.

4. **Develop a scaling up plan**: Your plan should include specific goals, objectives, and strategies. It should also identify the resources you will need, such as people, money, and equipment.

5. **Implement your plan**: Once you have a plan, it is time to start implementing it. This may involve hiring new employees, opening new locations, or expanding production.

6. **Monitor your progress and make adjustments as needed**: It is important to monitor your progress and make adjustments to your plan as needed. This will help you to stay on track and achieve your goals.

Here are some tips for scaling up successfully:

- **Focus on your core competencies**: It is important to focus on your core competencies when scaling up. This will help you to maintain quality control and efficiently allocate your resources.

- **Invest in the right people and technology**: You will need to invest in the right people and technology to support your growth. This includes hiring qualified employees and purchasing the necessary equipment and software.

- **Build a strong team**: A strong team is essential for scaling up successfully. Surround yourself with talented and experienced people who are committed to your vision.

- **Be prepared for challenges**: Scaling up is not without its challenges. Be prepared for unexpected setbacks and be willing to adapt your plans as needed.

The importance of scaling up

Scaling up is important for businesses to achieve sustained growth and success. It allows businesses to increase revenue, profitability, and market share. It can also lead to job creation and economic growth.

Here are some of the specific benefits of scaling up:

- **Increased revenue and profitability**: As a business scales up, it can serve more customers and produce more goods or services. This can lead to increased revenue and profitability.

- **Increased market share**: When a business scales up, it can reach more customers and expand into new markets. This can help the business to increase its market share.

- **Job creation**: As a business scales up, it needs to hire more employees. This can lead to job creation and economic growth.

- **Innovation**: Scaling up can also lead to innovation. When a business needs to serve more customers or produce more goods or services, it needs to find new and better ways to do so. This can lead to the development of new products, services, and processes.

- **Global competitiveness**: Scaling up can also help businesses to become more competitive in the global marketplace. When a business can produce goods or services at a larger scale, it can often do so more efficiently and at a lower cost. This can give the business an advantage over its competitors.

However, it is important to note that scaling up also comes with challenges. Businesses need to be careful to manage their growth effectively. They need to ensure that they have the resources and infrastructure in place to support their growth. They also need to make sure that they maintain quality control and customer satisfaction.

Overall, scaling up is an important part of business growth and success. By scaling up effectively, businesses can achieve their goals and make a positive impact on the economy.

Here are some examples of how scaling up can benefit businesses:

- A startup company that has developed a successful product might decide to scale up its production and sales operations to meet growing demand. This could lead to increased revenue, profitability, and market share. The company might also hire more employees, which would create jobs and boost the economy.

- A retail chain might decide to open new stores in new markets. This could help the company to reach more customers and increase its market share. The company might also hire more employees to operate the new stores.

- A software company might decide to develop new features and functionality for its product to attract more users. This could lead to increased revenue and profitability for the company. The company might also hire more employees to develop and maintain the new features.

- A manufacturing company might decide to build a new factory to increase its production capacity. This could help the company to meet growing demand for its products. The company might also hire more employees to operate the new factory.

The challenges of scaling up

Scaling up is the process of increasing the size or capacity of a business in order to achieve sustained growth. It can be a challenging process, but it is essential for businesses that want to succeed in the long term.

Here are some of the most common challenges of scaling up:

- **Maintaining quality control**: As a business grows, it can be difficult to maintain quality control. This is especially true if the business is expanding into new markets or launching new products or services.

- **Managing costs effectively**: Scaling up can be expensive. Businesses need to invest in new people, equipment, and infrastructure. They also need to manage their inventory and supply chain effectively.

- **Adapting to new markets**: When a business expands into new markets, it needs to adapt its products or services to meet the needs of the new customers. The business also needs to learn about the new market and its competitors.

- **Finding and retaining talent**: As a business grows, it needs to hire more employees. This can be difficult, especially in industries where there is a shortage of qualified workers. Businesses also need to retain their best employees by offering competitive salaries and benefits.

- **Maintaining culture**: As a business grows, it can be difficult to maintain its culture. This is especially true if the business is expanding into new markets or acquiring other businesses. Businesses need to be intentional about preserving their culture as they grow.

In addition to these general challenges, there are also specific challenges that businesses may face depending on their industry and business model. For example, a technology company may face the challenge of keeping up with rapid technological change. A retail company may face the challenge of managing a complex supply chain.

And a manufacturing company may face the challenge of meeting environmental regulations.

Despite the challenges, scaling up can be a very rewarding process. By planning carefully and managing their growth effectively, businesses can increase their chances of success.

Here are some tips for overcoming the challenges of scaling up:

- **Focus on your core competencies**: When you are scaling up, it is important to focus on your core competencies. This will help you to maintain quality control and efficiently allocate your resources.

- **Invest in the right people and technology**: As you grow, you will need to invest in the right people and technology to support your growth. This includes hiring qualified employees and purchasing the necessary equipment and software.

- **Build a strong team**: A strong team is essential for scaling up successfully. Surround yourself with talented and experienced people who are committed to your vision.

- **Be prepared for challenges**: Scaling up is not without its challenges. Be prepared for unexpected setbacks and be willing to adapt your plans as needed.

The scaling process
Planning and preparation

Planning and preparation are essential for successful scaling. By carefully planning and preparing for growth, businesses can minimize the risks associated with scaling and increase their chances of success.

Here are some key steps in planning and preparation for scaling:

1. **Define your goals**: What do you want to achieve by scaling up? Do you want to increase revenue, profitability, market share, or something else? Once you know your goals, you can develop a plan to achieve them.

2. **Assess your current capabilities**: What are your strengths and weaknesses? What resources do you have available? It is important to have a realistic understanding of your capabilities before you start scaling up.

3. **Identify your target market**: Who are you trying to reach with your products or services? Where are they located? What are

their needs and wants? Once you know your target market, you can develop strategies to reach them.

4. **Develop a scaling up plan**: Your plan should include specific goals, objectives, and strategies. It should also identify the resources you will need, such as people, money, and equipment.

5. **Monitor your progress and make adjustments as needed**: It is important to monitor your progress and make adjustments to your plan as needed. This will help you to stay on track and achieve your goals.

Here are some specific tips for planning and preparing for scaling:

*   **Start planning early**: The earlier you start planning for scaling, the better. This will give you time to identify and address any potential challenges.

*   **Be realistic**: It is important to be realistic about your goals and expectations. Scaling up takes time and effort. Don't expect to become a multinational overnight.

*   **Be flexible**: Things don't always go according to plan when scaling up. Be prepared to adjust your plans as needed.

- **Get help from others**: There are many resources available to help businesses scale up. This includes consultants, mentors, and other businesses that have successfully scaled up in the past.

Here are some examples of how businesses can plan and prepare for scaling:

- A startup company that has developed a successful product might decide to scale up its production and sales operations to meet growing demand. The company could start by developing a detailed plan that outlines its goals, objectives, and strategies. The plan should also identify the resources the company will need, such as people, money, and equipment.

- A retail chain that wants to expand into new markets might decide to start by conducting market research to identify the best locations for new stores. The company could then develop a plan for opening and operating the new stores. The plan should include timelines, budgets, and staffing requirements.

- A software company that wants to develop new features and functionality for its product might decide to start by gathering feedback from its customers. The company could then develop a product roadmap that prioritizes the new features and functionality. The company could also start hiring new employees to develop and maintain the new features.

- A manufacturing company that wants to increase its production capacity might decide to start by expanding its factory. The company could also develop a plan for improving its production efficiency. The company might also need to hire new employees to operate the expanded factory.

Implementation

Implementation in the scaling process is the act of putting your scaling plan into action. This includes hiring new employees, opening new locations, developing new products or services, and expanding your production capacity.

Implementation is the most important phase of the scaling process, as it is where you actually make your plans a reality. It is also the most challenging phase, as it requires careful execution and management.

Here are some key steps in the implementation phase of scaling:

1. **Communicate your plan to your team**: It is important to communicate your scaling plan to your team early on. This will help to get everyone on the same page and ensure that everyone is working towards the same goals.

2. **Set clear expectations**: Once you have communicated your plan to your team, it is important to set clear expectations for

everyone involved. This includes defining roles and responsibilities, setting deadlines, and establishing communication channels.

3. **Provide training and support**: As you implement your scaling plan, it is important to provide your team with the training and support they need to be successful. This includes providing them with the tools and resources they need, as well as offering them guidance and mentorship.

4. **Monitor your progress and make adjustments as needed**: It is important to monitor your progress and make adjustments to your plan as needed. This will help you to stay on track and achieve your goals.

Here are some tips for successful implementation in the scaling process:

- **Start small**: It is often best to start small when implementing a scaling plan. This will help you to identify and address any potential challenges before you scale up too quickly.

- **Be flexible**: Things don't always go according to plan when scaling up. Be prepared to adjust your plan as needed.

- **Get feedback from your team**: Get feedback from your team regularly to ensure that your scaling plan is working as expected.

- **Celebrate successes**: It is important to celebrate your successes along the way. This will help to keep your team motivated and engaged.

Here are some examples of implementation in the scaling process:

- A startup company that is scaling up its production and sales operations might start by hiring new employees to operate its new production lines. The company might also open new sales offices in new markets.

- A retail chain that is expanding into new markets might start by opening a small number of stores in the new markets. The company could then gradually open more stores as it learns more about the new markets and its customers.

- A software company that is developing new features and functionality for its product might start by releasing a beta version of the new features to a small group of users. The company could then gather feedback from the beta users and make improvements to the features before releasing them to all users.

- A manufacturing company that is increasing its production capacity might start by expanding its existing factory. The company could also purchase new equipment to improve its production efficiency.

Monitoring and evaluation

Monitoring and evaluation (M&E) is the process of collecting and analyzing data to track progress and assess the impact of a program or intervention. It is an essential part of the scaling process, as it allows businesses to identify and address any potential challenges early on and to ensure that their scaling efforts are having the desired impact.

There are two main types of M&E in the scaling process:

- **Process monitoring**: This involves tracking the implementation of the scaling plan and identifying any potential challenges. Process monitoring data can be used to make adjustments to the plan as needed.

- **Impact evaluation**: This involves measuring the impact of the scaling efforts on the business and its stakeholders. Impact evaluation data can be used to assess the success of the scaling process and to make decisions about future scaling efforts.

Here are some key steps in the M&E process for scaling:

1. **Define your goals**: What do you want to achieve with your M&E efforts? Do you want to track progress, identify

challenges, assess impact, or something else? Once you know your goals, you can develop a plan to collect and analyze the data you need.

2. **Select your indicators**: Indicators are specific measures that can be used to track progress and assess impact. When selecting indicators, it is important to choose indicators that are relevant to your goals, measurable, and achievable.

3. **Collect data**: Data can be collected through a variety of methods, such as surveys, interviews, focus groups, and observation. It is important to collect data on a regular basis so that you can track progress over time.

4. **Analyze data**: Once you have collected data, you need to analyze it to identify trends and patterns. This will help you to understand what is working well and what needs to be improved.

5. **Report findings**: It is important to report your findings to the appropriate stakeholders. This will help to keep everyone informed about the progress of the scaling efforts and to identify any areas where adjustments need to be made.

Here are some tips for successful M&E in the scaling process:

- **Start early**: It is important to start M&E early in the scaling process. This will allow you to identify and address any potential challenges early on.

- **Be flexible**: Things don't always go according to plan when scaling up. Be prepared to adjust your M&E plan as needed.

- **Get feedback from your team**: Get feedback from your team regularly to ensure that your M&E plan is working as expected.

- **Use data to make decisions**: Use the data you collect to make informed decisions about your scaling efforts.

Here are some examples of M&E in the scaling process:

- A startup company that is scaling up its production and sales operations might track the number of new products or services launched, the number of new customers acquired, and the amount of revenue generated. The company could also use surveys to collect feedback from customers about their satisfaction with the company's products or services.

- A retail chain that is expanding into new markets might track the number of new stores opened, the sales volume of each new store, and the customer satisfaction ratings of each new store. The company could also use interviews to collect feedback from customers about their experience shopping at the new stores.

- A software company that is developing new features and functionality for its product might track the number of new features released, the number of users who adopt the new features, and the satisfaction of users with the new features. The company could also use focus groups to collect feedback from users about the new features.

- A manufacturing company that is increasing its production capacity might track the number of new production lines added, the amount of output produced by each new production line, and the quality of the output produced by each new production line. The company could also use observation to collect data about the efficiency of the new production lines.

The key factors for successful scaling up

A clear vision and strategy

A clear vision and strategy are two of the most important key factors for successful scaling up. A vision is a statement of what the business wants to achieve in the long term, while a strategy is a plan for how the business will achieve its vision.

A clear vision is important for scaling up because it provides a sense of direction and purpose. It helps to keep everyone aligned and focused on the same goals. A clear vision is also important for attracting and retaining top talent, as people are more likely to want to work for a company that has a clear vision for the future.

A strong strategy is important for scaling up because it provides a roadmap for how the business will achieve its vision. It identifies the key steps that the business needs to take in order to grow and succeed. A strong strategy also helps to ensure that the business is making the most of its resources and opportunities.

Here are some tips for developing a clear vision and strategy for scaling up:

- **Start with your core values**: What are the core values of your business? What do you stand for? Your vision and strategy should be aligned with your core values.

- **Understand your customers**: Who are your customers? What are their needs and wants? Your vision and strategy should be focused on meeting the needs of your customers.

- **Define your goals**: What do you want to achieve with your scaling up efforts? Do you want to increase revenue, market share, or something else? Once you know your goals, you can develop a strategy to achieve them.

- **Develop a roadmap**: What steps do you need to take in order to achieve your goals? Develop a roadmap that outlines the key steps and milestones.

- **Be flexible**: Things don't always go according to plan when scaling up. Be prepared to adjust your vision and strategy as needed.

Here are some examples of how a clear vision and strategy can help businesses to scale up successfully:

- A startup company that has developed a successful product might have a vision to become the leading provider of that product in the world. The company's strategy might involve expanding into new markets, launching new products or services, and acquiring competitors.

- A retail chain that wants to expand into new markets might have a vision to become a global retailer. The company's strategy might involve opening new stores in new countries, developing a strong online presence, and partnering with local businesses.

- A software company that wants to develop new features and functionality for its product might have a vision to become the leading provider of software for a particular industry. The company's strategy might involve investing in research and development, partnering with other companies, and acquiring competitors.

- A manufacturing company that wants to increase its production capacity might have a vision to become the world's largest manufacturer of a particular product. The company's strategy might involve building new factories, expanding its existing factories, and investing in new equipment.

A strong leadership team

A strong leadership team is another key factor for successful scaling up. A strong leadership team is one that is composed of experienced and talented individuals who are committed to the company's vision and strategy.

A strong leadership team is important for scaling up because it provides the guidance and direction that the company needs to grow and succeed. A strong leadership team is also important for managing the challenges of scaling up, such as maintaining quality control, managing costs effectively, and adapting to new markets.

Here are some of the key characteristics of a strong leadership team:

- **Experience**: The leadership team should have experience in scaling up businesses. This experience is essential for managing the challenges of scaling up and for making informed decisions.

- **Talent**: The leadership team should be composed of talented individuals who have the skills and knowledge necessary to lead the company to success.

- **Commitment**: The leadership team should be committed to the company's vision and strategy. This commitment is essential for keeping everyone aligned and focused on the same goals.

Here are some tips for building a strong leadership team for scaling up:

- **Hire the right people**: When hiring for your leadership team, look for people who have the experience, talent, and commitment that you need.

- **Develop your team**: Invest in the development of your
  leadership team. This will help them to grow and develop the
  skills and knowledge they need to be successful.

- **Create a culture of teamwork**: Create a culture of teamwork
  and collaboration within your leadership team. This will help
  them to work together effectively and to achieve the
  company's goals.

Here are some examples of how a strong leadership team can help
businesses to scale up successfully:

- A startup company that has developed a successful product
  might have a leadership team with experience in launching and
  scaling businesses. The leadership team could use their
  experience to guide the company through the process of
  scaling up its production and sales operations.

- A retail chain that wants to expand into new markets might
  have a leadership team with experience in expanding into new
  markets. The leadership team could use their experience to
  help the company to select the right markets to expand into,
  to develop a plan for expansion, and to execute the plan
  successfully.

- A software company that wants to develop new features and
  functionality for its product might have a leadership team with
  experience in developing and launching new products. The

leadership team could use their experience to help the company to develop a roadmap for the new features, to manage the development process, and to launch the new features successfully.

- A manufacturing company that wants to increase its production capacity might have a leadership team with experience in expanding factories and building new factories. The leadership team could use their experience to help the company to develop a plan for increasing its production capacity, to manage the expansion process, and to execute the plan successfully.

Adequate resources

Adequate resources is another key factor for successful scaling up. Resources include people, money, and equipment.

People: Businesses need to have the right people in place to support their growth. This includes hiring new employees, training existing employees, and developing a strong leadership team.

Money: Businesses need to have the financial resources to support their growth. This includes investing in new equipment, expanding into new markets, and developing new products or services.

Equipment: Businesses need to have the right equipment to support their growth. This includes investing in new production lines, new software, and new IT infrastructure.

Here are some tips for ensuring that you have adequate resources for scaling up:

- **Plan for growth**: When developing your scaling plan, be sure to factor in the resources you will need. This includes the number of people you will need to hire, the amount of money you will need to invest, and the equipment you will need to purchase.

- **Invest wisely**: Be sure to invest your resources wisely. This means focusing on the resources that are most essential for your growth.

- **Seek outside funding**: If you need additional resources, consider seeking outside funding from investors or banks.

Here are some examples of how adequate resources can help businesses to scale up successfully:

- A startup company that has developed a successful product might need to hire new employees to support its growing sales and production operations. The company might also need to invest in new equipment to increase its production capacity.

- A retail chain that wants to expand into new markets might need to hire new employees to staff its new stores. The company might also need to invest in new inventory and marketing campaigns.

- A software company that wants to develop new features and functionality for its product might need to hire new software developers and testers. The company might also need to invest in new development tools and infrastructure.

- A manufacturing company that wants to increase its production capacity might need to hire new factory workers. The company might also need to invest in new production lines and equipment.

By ensuring that they have adequate resources in place, businesses can increase their chances of successfully scaling up.

A culture of innovation and learning

A culture of innovation and learning is another key factor for successful scaling up. A culture of innovation and learning is one that encourages employees to come up with new ideas, to experiment, and to learn from their mistakes.

A culture of innovation and learning is important for scaling up because it allows businesses to adapt to new markets and to develop new products or services. It also helps businesses to stay ahead of the competition and to remain innovative.

Here are some of the key characteristics of a culture of innovation and learning:

- **Openness to new ideas**: Employees should feel comfortable sharing their new ideas, even if they are not fully formed.

- **Encouragement of experimentation**: Employees should feel encouraged to experiment with new ideas and approaches.

- **Tolerance for failure**: Failure is a natural part of the innovation process. Employees should feel comfortable failing and learning from their mistakes.

- **Investment in learning and development**: Businesses should invest in learning and development opportunities for their employees. This will help them to develop the skills and knowledge they need to be innovative.

Here are some tips for creating a culture of innovation and learning:

- **Lead by example**: Leaders should model the behavior they want to see in their employees. This means being open to new ideas, encouraging experimentation, and learning from mistakes.

- **Provide opportunities for collaboration**: Create opportunities for employees to collaborate with each other and to share their ideas. This can be done through team meetings, workshops, and hackathons.

- **Celebrate successes**: When employees come up with new ideas and achieve success, celebrate their accomplishments. This will help to motivate them and to encourage others to be innovative.

Here are some examples of how a culture of innovation and learning can help businesses to scale up successfully:

- A startup company that has developed a successful product might be constantly innovating to improve its product and to develop new products. The company's culture of innovation and learning would encourage employees to come up with new ideas and to experiment with new approaches.

- A retail chain that wants to expand into new markets might need to learn about the new markets and to adapt its products and services to meet the needs of the new customers. The company's culture of innovation and learning would encourage employees to learn about the new markets and to come up with new ideas for adapting the company's products and services.

- A software company that wants to develop new features and functionality for its product might need to learn about new technologies and to experiment with new approaches. The company's culture of innovation and learning would encourage employees to learn about new technologies and to experiment with new approaches.

- A manufacturing company that wants to increase its production capacity might need to develop new production methods and to experiment with new technologies. The company's culture of innovation and learning would encourage employees to develop new production methods and to experiment with new technologies.

A supportive environment

A supportive environment is another key factor for successful scaling up. This includes having supportive stakeholders, such as investors, customers, and partners. It also includes having a supportive ecosystem, such as access to capital, talent, and resources.

A supportive environment is important for scaling up because it provides the business with the support it needs to grow and succeed. Supportive stakeholders can provide the business with funding, advice, and mentorship. A supportive ecosystem can provide the business with access to the resources it needs, such as capital, talent, and infrastructure.

Here are some of the key elements of a supportive environment for scaling up:

- **Supportive stakeholders**: Businesses need to have supportive stakeholders, such as investors, customers, and partners. These stakeholders can provide the business with the resources, advice, and support it needs to grow and succeed.

- **Supportive ecosystem**: Businesses need to have access to a supportive ecosystem. This includes having access to capital, talent, and infrastructure. A supportive ecosystem can help businesses to scale up more easily and effectively.

Here are some tips for creating a supportive environment for scaling up:

- **Build relationships with key stakeholders**: Build relationships with key stakeholders, such as investors, customers, and partners. These relationships will be essential for getting the support you need to scale up.

- **Get involved in the startup community**: Get involved in the startup community. This will give you access to resources and support, and it will also help you to build relationships with potential investors, customers, and partners.

- **Create a positive work environment**: Create a positive work environment for your employees. This will help to attract and retain top talent, and it will also create a culture of innovation and learning.

Here are some examples of how a supportive environment can help businesses to scale up successfully:

- A startup company that has developed a successful product might have supportive investors who are willing to provide the company with the funding it needs to grow and expand. The company might also have supportive customers who are willing to provide feedback and help the company to improve its product.

- A retail chain that wants to expand into new markets might have supportive partners who can help the company to set up new stores and to market its products and services in the new markets. The company might also have access to a supportive ecosystem that includes government agencies, chambers of commerce, and other organizations that can provide assistance to businesses that are expanding.

- A software company that wants to develop new features and functionality for its product might have supportive customers who are willing to beta test the new features and provide feedback. The company might also have access to a supportive ecosystem that includes technology incubators and accelerators that can provide assistance to software companies that are developing new products and services.

- A manufacturing company that wants to increase its production capacity might have supportive investors who are willing to provide the company with the funding it needs to build new factories and purchase new equipment. The company might also have access to a supportive ecosystem that includes government agencies and economic development organizations that can provide assistance to businesses that are expanding.

By creating a supportive environment, businesses can increase their chances of successfully scaling up and achieving their goals.

In addition to the above, here are some other ways to create a supportive environment for scaling up:

- **Create a clear vision and strategy.** This will help to keep everyone aligned and focused on the same goals.

- **Build a strong team.** A strong team is essential for scaling up successfully. Surround yourself with talented and experienced people who are committed to your vision.

- **Be flexible and adaptable.** Things don't always go according to plan when scaling up. Be prepared to adjust your plans as needed.

- **Celebrate successes.** It is important to celebrate successes along the way. This will help to keep everyone motivated and engaged.

The different scaling strategies

Organic growth

Organic growth is a scaling strategy that involves growing your business without relying on external funding or acquisitions. This is the most common type of scaling strategy, and it is the one that is most often used by small businesses.

Organic growth can be achieved through a variety of strategies, including:

- **Increasing sales to existing customers**: This can be done by offering new products or services, expanding into new markets, or increasing marketing efforts.

- **Acquiring new customers**: This can be done through marketing, sales, and public relations efforts.

- **Improving operational efficiency**: This can be done by streamlining processes, investing in technology, and reducing costs.

- **Developing new products and services**: This can help to expand your customer base and increase sales.

- **Expanding into new markets:** This can help to grow your business and reach new customers.

Organic growth is a gradual process, but it is also a sustainable one. When you grow your business organically, you are building a solid foundation for long-term success.

Here are some examples of organic growth:

- A retail store that opens new locations.

- A software company that develops new products or features.

- A restaurant that expands its menu and hours of operation.

- A consulting firm that hires new consultants and expands its services.

- A manufacturing company that builds new factories or invests in new equipment.

Organic growth is a good option for businesses that want to grow at a steady pace and that have a strong competitive advantage. It is also a good option for businesses that do not have access to external funding or that do not want to be acquired by another company.

Here are some tips for successful organic growth:

- **Focus on your core competencies**: What are you good at? What do your customers value? Focus on growing your business in areas where you have a competitive advantage.

- **Invest in your people**: Your employees are your most important asset. Invest in their training and development so that they can help you to grow your business.

- **Build relationships with your customers**: Get to know your customers and what they want. Build relationships with them so that they become loyal customers for life.

- **Market your business effectively**: Let people know about your business and what you have to offer. Invest in marketing and advertising to reach new customers and grow your sales.

- **Be patient and persistent**: Organic growth takes time and effort. Don't get discouraged if you don't see results immediately. Just keep focused on your goals and keep working hard.

Acquisitions

Acquisitions is a scaling strategy that involves growing your business by acquiring other businesses. This is a faster way to grow than organic growth, but it is also more complex and risky.

Acquisitions can be used to achieve a variety of goals, such as:

- **Expanding into new markets**: Acquiring a business in a new market can give you instant access to that market and its customers.

- **Adding new products or services**: Acquiring a business that offers complementary products or services can help you to expand your product or service offerings and reach new customers.

- **Gaining market share**: Acquiring a competitor can help you to gain market share and increase your profitability.

- **Acquiring key talent**: Acquiring a business with a team of skilled and experienced employees can help you to quickly build your own team and accelerate your growth.

- **Acquiring intellectual property**: Acquiring a business with valuable intellectual property, such as patents or trademarks, can give you a competitive advantage.

Acquisitions can be a complex and risky process, but it can also be a very effective way to scale your business quickly. If you are considering an acquisition, it is important to carefully evaluate the business you are considering acquiring and to have a detailed plan for integrating the two businesses.

Here are some examples of acquisitions:

- A social media company acquiring a messaging app.

- A software company acquiring a startup with a promising new technology.

- A retail chain acquiring a competitor.

- A manufacturing company acquiring a supplier.

- A healthcare company acquiring a pharmaceutical company.

Acquisitions can be a good option for businesses that want to grow quickly and that have the financial resources to do so. It is also a good option for businesses that want to expand into new markets or add new products or services to their offerings.

Here are some tips for successful acquisitions:

- **Do your homework**: Carefully evaluate the business you are considering acquiring. This includes understanding its financial performance, its competitive landscape, and its management team.

- **Have a clear plan**: Develop a detailed plan for how you will integrate the two businesses. This includes addressing issues such as culture, branding, and operations.

- **Be prepared to pay a premium**: Good businesses are not cheap. Be prepared to pay a premium for a business that is a good fit for your company and that will help you to achieve your goals.

- **Get the right team in place**: Assemble a team of experienced professionals to help you with the acquisition process. This includes lawyers, accountants, and consultants.

Partnerships

Partnerships are a scaling strategy that involves partnering with other businesses to achieve common goals. Partnerships can be a great way to expand your reach, gain access to new resources, and learn from other businesses.

There are many different types of partnerships, such as:

- **Joint ventures**: A joint venture is a new business entity that is created by two or more businesses. Joint ventures can be used to develop new products or services, enter new markets, or expand into new business areas.

- **Strategic alliances**: A strategic alliance is a partnership between two or more businesses that agree to work together on specific projects or initiatives. Strategic alliances can be used to share resources, collaborate on research and development, or market and sell each other's products or services.

- **Channel partnerships**: A channel partnership is a partnership between a business and a channel partner, such as a distributor, retailer, or reseller. Channel partnerships can be used to expand your reach and make your products or services more accessible to customers.

- **Technology partnerships**: A technology partnership is a partnership between a business and a technology company. Technology partnerships can be used to develop new products or services, integrate your products or services with other products or services, or gain access to new technologies.

Partnerships can be a great way to scale your business, but it is important to choose the right partners and to carefully structure the partnership. It is also important to have a clear understanding of the roles and responsibilities of each partner.

Here are some examples of partnerships:

- A software company partnering with a cloud computing company to offer its products or services on the cloud.
- A retail chain partnering with a credit card company to offer its customers a co-branded credit card.
- A manufacturing company partnering with a supplier to develop new products or reduce costs.
- A healthcare company partnering with a pharmaceutical company to develop new drugs or treatments.
- A financial services company partnering with a technology company to develop new financial products or services.

Partnerships can be a good option for businesses of all sizes. For small businesses, partnerships can be a way to gain access to resources and expertise that they would not be able to afford on their own. For large businesses, partnerships can be a way to expand their reach and enter new markets.

Here are some tips for successful partnerships:

- **Choose the right partners**: Choose partners that have complementary products or services and that share your values and goals.

- **Structure the partnership carefully**: Have a clear understanding of the roles and responsibilities of each partner and how the partnership will be managed.

- **Set clear expectations**: Communicate your goals and expectations to your partners early on.

- **Be flexible and adaptable**: Things don't always go according to plan when working with partners. Be prepared to adjust your plans as needed.

- **Communicate regularly**: Communicate regularly with your partners to ensure that the partnership is on track and to address any potential issues.

Franchising

Franchising is a scaling strategy that involves franchising your business model to other entrepreneurs, known as franchisees. The franchisor provides the franchisee with the training, support, and resources they need to operate a successful franchise. In return, the franchisee pays the franchisor a franchise fee and ongoing royalties.

Franchising is a great way to scale your business quickly and efficiently. It allows you to leverage the resources and expertise of your franchisees to grow your brand and reach new markets.

There are two main types of franchises:

- **Product distribution franchises**: These franchises sell the franchisor's products, such as fast food restaurants and convenience stores.

- **Business format franchises**: These franchises use the franchisor's business model, including its branding, operating procedures, and marketing materials. Examples of business format franchises include hotels, fitness gyms, and hair salons.

Franchising can be a good option for businesses that have a proven business model and that are ready to expand quickly. It is also a good option for businesses that want to enter new markets but do not want to invest in opening and operating their own locations.

Here are some examples of franchises:

- McDonald's
- Subway
- Starbucks

- Domino's Pizza

- KFC

- Hilton Hotels

- Marriott Hotels

- Holiday Inn

- 7-Eleven

- Circle K

- Anytime Fitness

- Curves

- Jiffy Lube

Here are some tips for successful franchising:

- **Have a proven business model**: Your business model should be proven and profitable before you start franchising.

- **Develop a comprehensive franchise system**: This includes developing franchise documentation, training programs, and support systems.

- **Choose the right franchisees**: Look for franchisees who have the necessary experience, financial resources, and business acumen to operate a successful franchise.

- **Provide ongoing support to your franchisees**: Your franchisees will need your support to be successful. Provide them with training, marketing assistance, and other resources.

- **Monitor your franchisees**: It is important to monitor your franchisees to ensure that they are meeting your standards and operating their businesses in a consistent manner.

The risks of scaling up
Loss of control

Loss of control is one of the biggest risks of scaling up. As a business grows, it can become more difficult to maintain control over all aspects of the business. This can lead to problems such as:

- **Decreased quality**: As a business grows, it can become more difficult to maintain the same level of quality in its products or services. This is because it can be more difficult to train and supervise employees, and to ensure that quality standards are being met.

- **Increased costs**: As a business grows, its costs will also increase. This is because the business will need to invest in new equipment, facilities, and employees. If the business is not able to manage its costs effectively, this can lead to profitability problems.

- **Cultural challenges**: As a business grows, it can become more difficult to maintain a strong culture. This is because the business will have a more diverse workforce, and it will be more difficult to communicate and collaborate effectively.

- **Regulatory compliance**: As a business grows, it will become subject to more regulations. If the business is not able to comply with these regulations, this can lead to fines, penalties, and other problems.

To mitigate the risk of loss of control, businesses need to have a plan in place for scaling up. This plan should include strategies for maintaining quality, managing costs, maintaining culture, and complying with regulations. Businesses also need to be prepared to adapt their plans as needed.

Here are some tips for mitigating the risk of loss of control when scaling up:

- **Invest in training and development**: Invest in training and development programs for your employees. This will help to ensure that they have the skills and knowledge they need to perform their jobs effectively.

- **Implement quality control measures**: Implement quality control measures to ensure that your products or services are meeting your standards. This may involve conducting inspections, audits, and customer surveys.

- **Set clear expectations**: Set clear expectations for your employees and communicate them regularly. This will help to ensure that everyone is aligned and working towards the same goals.

- **Use technology to your advantage**: Use technology to automate tasks and streamline processes. This will free up your time and resources so that you can focus on more important things.

- **Delegate tasks**: Delegate tasks to your employees and trust them to get the job done. This will free up your time so that you can focus on the strategic aspects of your business.

- **Hire experienced managers**: Hire experienced managers to help you manage your business. Experienced managers will have the skills and knowledge necessary to help you scale up your business successfully.

Culture clashes

Culture clashes are another risk of scaling up. As a business grows, it may become more difficult to maintain a consistent culture. This is because the business will have a more diverse workforce, and it will be more difficult to communicate and collaborate effectively.

Culture clashes can lead to a number of problems, including:

- **Decreased morale**: Employees who feel like they don't fit in with the company culture are more likely to have low morale. This can lead to decreased productivity and increased turnover.

- **Communication challenges**: Employees from different cultures may have different communication styles. This can lead to misunderstandings and conflicts.

- **Decreased collaboration**: Employees from different cultures may have different work styles. This can make it difficult for them to collaborate effectively.

- **Increased conflict**: Culture clashes can lead to increased conflict between employees. This can disrupt the workplace and make it difficult to get work done.

To mitigate the risk of culture clashes, businesses need to be proactive. Businesses need to create a culture that is inclusive and welcoming to all employees. Businesses also need to provide training on cultural awareness and communication to their employees.

Here are some tips for mitigating the risk of culture clashes when scaling up:

- **Define your company culture**: What are your company's values and beliefs? What kind of work environment do you want to create? Once you have defined your company culture, communicate it to your employees and make sure that everyone is aligned.

- **Hire for culture fit**: When hiring new employees, look for candidates who are a good fit for your company culture. This doesn't mean that you should only hire people who are just like you. Rather, you should hire people who share your values and who will contribute to a positive work environment.

- **Provide training on cultural awareness and communication**: Provide training on cultural awareness and communication to your employees. This will help them to understand and appreciate different cultures, and to communicate effectively with people from different backgrounds.

- **Encourage cross-cultural collaboration**: Encourage cross-cultural collaboration within your company. This will help employees to learn from each other and to appreciate different perspectives.

- **Celebrate diversity**: Celebrate diversity within your company. This will help to create a more inclusive and welcoming work environment.

Financial problems

Financial problems are another risk of scaling up. As a business grows, its costs will also increase. This is because the business will need to invest in new equipment, facilities, and employees. If the business is not able to manage its costs effectively, this can lead to profitability problems.

Other financial risks of scaling up include:

- **Cash flow problems**: As a business grows, it may experience cash flow problems. This is because the business may need to spend money on growth initiatives before it starts to see a return on its investment.

- **Debt problems**: Businesses that scale up quickly may need to take on debt to finance their growth. This can lead to debt problems if the business is not able to generate enough revenue to service its debt.

- **Profitability problems**: As a business grows, its profitability may decline. This is because the business may need to invest in new markets and new products, which can reduce its margins in the short term.

To mitigate the risk of financial problems, businesses need to have a sound financial plan in place. This plan should include strategies for managing costs, generating cash flow, and managing debt. Businesses also need to be prepared to adjust their plans as needed.

Here are some tips for mitigating the risk of financial problems when scaling up:

- **Create a financial plan**: Create a detailed financial plan that includes projections for revenue, expenses, cash flow, and debt. This will help you to identify potential financial problems and to develop strategies for mitigating them.

- **Monitor your finances closely**: Monitor your finances closely and make adjustments to your plan as needed. This will help you to avoid financial problems before they occur.

- **Seek professional advice**: If you are not sure how to manage your finances effectively, seek professional advice from an accountant or financial advisor.

Operational challenges

Operational challenges are another risk of scaling up. As a business grows, it can become more difficult to manage its operations effectively. This is because the business will have more employees, more products or services, and more customers.

Operational challenges can lead to a number of problems, including:

- **Decreased quality:** As a business grows, it can become more difficult to maintain the same level of quality in its products or services. This is because it can be more difficult to train and supervise employees, and to ensure that quality standards are being met.

- **Increased costs:** As a business grows, its costs will also increase. This is because the business will need to invest in new equipment, facilities, and employees. If the business is not able to manage its costs effectively, this can lead to profitability problems.

- **Decreased efficiency:** As a business grows, it can become less efficient. This is because it can be more difficult to coordinate the activities of different departments and employees.

- **Customer service problems**: As a business grows, it can become more difficult to provide good customer service. This is because it can be more difficult to respond to customer inquiries and to resolve customer problems.

To mitigate the risk of operational challenges, businesses need to have a plan in place for scaling up. This plan should include strategies for maintaining quality, managing costs, improving efficiency, and providing good customer service. Businesses also need to be prepared to adapt their plans as needed.

Here are some tips for mitigating the risk of operational challenges when scaling up:

- **Invest in technology**: Technology can help you to manage your operations more effectively. For example, you can use customer relationship management (CRM) software to track customer interactions, and you can use enterprise resource planning (ERP) software to manage your finances and inventory.

- **Streamline your processes**: Take some time to review your business processes and see if there are any ways to streamline them. This can help to improve efficiency and reduce costs.

- **Hire experienced managers**: Hire experienced managers to help you manage your operations. Experienced managers will have the skills and knowledge necessary to help you scale up your business successfully.

- **Delegate tasks**: Delegate tasks to your employees and trust them to get the job done. This will free up your time so that you can focus on the strategic aspects of your business.

How to mitigate the risks of scaling up
Careful planning and preparation

Careful planning and preparation is essential for mitigating the risks of scaling up. Businesses need to have a clear plan in place for how they will scale up, and they need to be prepared to adapt their plans as needed.

Here are some specific steps that businesses can take to carefully plan and prepare for scaling up:

1. **Define your goals**: What do you want to achieve by scaling up? Do you want to increase your revenue, market share, or customer base? Once you know your goals, you can develop a plan to achieve them.

2. **Assess your current state**: What are your strengths and weaknesses? What resources do you have available? What challenges are you likely to face? Once you have a good understanding of your current state, you can start to develop a plan to address your weaknesses and challenges.

3. **Develop a scaling strategy**: Your scaling strategy should outline how you will achieve your goals. This should include strategies for managing costs, increasing sales, and expanding into new markets.

4. **Create a financial plan**: Your financial plan should project your revenue, expenses, cash flow, and debt. This will help you to identify potential financial problems and to develop strategies for mitigating them.

5. **Put your plan into action**: Once you have a plan in place, it's time to start putting it into action. Be prepared to adjust your plan as needed as you learn more about your business and the market.

It is also important to involve your employees in the planning process. Employees can provide valuable insights into the challenges and opportunities of scaling up. By involving employees in the planning process, you can create a more buy-in and support for scaling up.

Here are some additional tips for careful planning and preparation when scaling up:

- **Seek professional advice**: If you are not sure how to develop a scaling plan or financial plan, seek professional advice from an accountant, financial advisor, or business consultant.

- **Get buy-in from stakeholders**: It is important to get buy-in from stakeholders, such as investors, customers, and suppliers, before scaling up. This will help to ensure that everyone is aligned and supportive of your plans.

- **Be flexible and adaptable**: Things don't always go according to plan when scaling up. Be prepared to adjust your plans as needed as you learn more about your business and the market.

Strong leadership

Strong leadership is essential for mitigating the risks of scaling up. As a business grows, it becomes more complex and challenging to manage. Strong leaders can provide the vision, guidance, and support that businesses need to scale up successfully.

Here are some specific ways that strong leadership can help to mitigate the risks of scaling up:

- **Communicate the vision and strategy**: Strong leaders can communicate the vision and strategy for scaling up clearly and effectively to all employees. This helps to ensure that everyone is aligned and working towards the same goals.

- **Build a strong team**: Strong leaders can build a strong team of experienced and talented employees. This team is essential for executing the scaling strategy and overcoming challenges along the way.

- **Create a culture of innovation and learning**: Strong leaders can create a culture of innovation and learning within the organization. This culture is essential for businesses to adapt to change and grow.

- **Be decisive and take action**: Strong leaders are decisive and take action even in the face of uncertainty. This is essential for businesses to move quickly and capitalize on opportunities.

- **Be supportive and approachable**: Strong leaders are supportive and approachable. They create an environment where employees feel comfortable sharing ideas and feedback. This is essential for businesses to learn from their mistakes and improve.

Here are some additional tips for strong leadership when scaling up:

- **Be humble and open to feedback**: No one is perfect, and even the best leaders make mistakes. Be humble and open to feedback from your team. This will help you to learn and grow.

- **Celebrate successes**: It is important to celebrate successes along the way. This will help to keep your team motivated and engaged.

- **Be patient and persistent**: Scaling up takes time and effort. Don't get discouraged if you don't see results immediately. Just keep focused on your goals and keep working hard.

Adequate resources

Adequate resources are essential for mitigating the risks of scaling up. As a business grows, it needs more resources to support its growth. These resources include financial resources, human resources, and technological resources.

Financial resources are needed to invest in new equipment, facilities, and employees. It is also important to have a cash flow cushion to cover unexpected expenses.

Human resources are needed to manage and execute the scaling strategy. Businesses need to hire experienced and talented employees in key areas such as sales, marketing, and operations.

Technological resources are needed to support the business's growth. Businesses may need to invest in new software, hardware, and other technologies.

Here are some specific steps that businesses can take to ensure that they have adequate resources for scaling up:

- **Develop a financial plan**: Your financial plan should project your revenue, expenses, cash flow, and debt. This will help you to identify potential financial needs and to develop strategies for meeting those needs.

- **Assess your human resources**: Do you have the right people in place to support your growth? Do you need to hire new employees or train existing employees?

- **Evaluate your technological needs**: Do you have the right technologies in place to support your growth? Do you need to invest in new software, hardware, or other technologies?

It is also important to have a plan for managing your resources effectively. As a business grows, it can become more difficult to manage resources efficiently. Businesses need to have systems and processes in place to track and manage their resources effectively.

Here are some additional tips for ensuring adequate resources when scaling up:

- **Seek funding**: If you need financial resources to support your growth, seek funding from investors or lenders.

- **Invest in training and development**: Invest in training and development programs for your employees. This will help to ensure that they have the skills and knowledge they need to support the business's growth.

- **Outsource tasks**: If you do not have the resources to manage all tasks in-house, consider outsourcing some tasks to third-party providers. This can help you to free up your resources so that you can focus on the most important tasks.

A culture of communication and collaboration

A culture of communication and collaboration is essential for mitigating the risks of scaling up. As a business grows, it becomes more complex and challenging to manage. A culture of communication and collaboration can help businesses to:

- **Improve decision-making**: When employees communicate and collaborate effectively, they are able to share ideas and perspectives, which can lead to better decision-making.

- **Reduce errors**: When employees communicate and collaborate effectively, they are less likely to make mistakes. This is because they are able to ask questions, get feedback, and learn from each other.

- **Improve efficiency**: When employees communicate and collaborate effectively, they are able to work together more efficiently. This is because they are able to coordinate their efforts and avoid duplication of work.

- **Boost morale**: When employees feel like they are part of a team and that their voices are heard, they are more likely to be motivated and engaged. This can lead to increased productivity and improved performance.

Here are some specific steps that businesses can take to create a culture of communication and collaboration:

- **Set clear expectations**: Communicate your expectations for communication and collaboration to all employees. This includes expectations for how employees should communicate with each other, with customers, and with suppliers.

- **Provide opportunities for communication and collaboration**: Create opportunities for employees to communicate and collaborate with each other. This can be done through team meetings, workshops, and social events.

- **Encourage open and honest communication**: Encourage employees to communicate openly and honestly with each other. This means creating a safe environment where employees feel comfortable sharing their ideas, even if they are not fully formed.

- **Celebrate successes**: When employees communicate and collaborate effectively, celebrate their successes. This will help to reinforce the importance of communication and collaboration.

Here are some additional tips for creating a culture of communication and collaboration when scaling up:

- **Use technology to your advantage**: There are a number of technology tools that can help businesses to improve communication and collaboration. For example, you can use video conferencing software to connect employees in different locations, and you can use project management software to help employees track and manage projects collaboratively.

- **Encourage feedback**: Encourage employees to give and receive feedback. This will help employees to learn from each other and to improve their performance.

- **Be a role model**: Set an example for your employees by communicating and collaborating effectively yourself.

A willingness to learn from mistakes

A willingness to learn from mistakes is essential for mitigating the risks of scaling up. As a business grows, it will inevitably make mistakes. However, businesses can learn from their mistakes and become stronger as a result.

Here are some specific ways that businesses can learn from their mistakes:

- **Identify the mistake:** The first step to learning from a mistake is to identify it. This can be difficult, as it can be painful to admit that you have made a mistake. However, it is important to identify the mistake so that you can learn from it.

- **Analyze the mistake:** Once you have identified the mistake, take some time to analyze it. What went wrong? Why did it go wrong? What can you do to prevent it from happening again?

- **Develop a plan to address the mistake:** Once you have analyzed the mistake, develop a plan to address it. This plan may involve changing your processes, training your employees, or investing in new technology.

- **Implement the plan and monitor the results:** Once you have developed a plan, implement it and monitor the results. This will help you to ensure that the plan is effective and that the mistake is not repeated.

Here are some additional tips for learning from mistakes when scaling up:

- **Create a culture of learning**: Create a culture where employees feel comfortable admitting their mistakes and sharing them with others. This will help to ensure that everyone learns from their mistakes.

- **Celebrate successes**: When employees learn from their mistakes, celebrate their successes. This will help to reinforce the importance of learning from mistakes.

- **Be patient and persistent**: Learning from mistakes takes time and effort. Don't get discouraged if you don't see results immediately. Just keep focused on learning from your mistakes and improving your business.

By being willing to learn from their mistakes, businesses can mitigate the risks of scaling up and increase their chances of success.

Here are some examples of how businesses can learn from their mistakes:

- If a business launches a new product that fails to gain market traction, the business can learn from its mistakes and develop better products in the future.

- If a business experiences a data breach, the business can learn from its mistakes and improve its security measures to prevent future data breaches.

- If a business expands into a new market and fails to be successful, the business can learn from its mistakes and develop a better strategy for expanding into new markets in the future.